❧ History *of* Britain ❧

The Tudors

1485 to 1603

G000150163

Andrew Langley

HAMLYN

HISTORY OF BRITAIN – TUDORS
was produced for Hamlyn Children's Books
by Lionheart Books, London.
Editor: Lionel Bender
Designer: Ben White
Picture Researcher: Jennie Karrach
Media Conversion and Typesetting:
    Peter MacDonald and Una Macnamara

Educational Consultant: Jane Shuter
Editorial Advisors: Andrew Farrow, Paul Shuter

Production Controller: Linda Spillane
Managing Editor: David Riley

First Published in Great Britain in 1993
by Hamlyn Children's Books,
an imprint of Reed Children's Books Limited,
Michelin House, 81 Fulham Road, London SW3 6RB,
and Auckland, Melbourne, Singapore and Toronto.
Reprinted in 1994

ISBN 0 600 58028 8 (PB)   ISBN 0 600 58029 6 (HB)

British Library Cataloguing-in-Publication Data. A catalogue
record for this book is available from the British Library.

Acknowledgements
Photo credits: By courtesy of the National Portrait Gallery, London:
pages: 6, 7, 14, 16, 39, 43 (top left and right). The Royal Collection ©
1993 Her Majesty the Queen: pages 9, 13. From the Castle Howard
Collection, Yorks: page 10 left. The Public Record Office: page 10
right. Michael Holford: pages 15 (top), 30. The Mansell Collection:
pages 15 (bottom), 17 (bottom), 20 (left), 23, 25, 26, 29, 32, 34, 35,
37 (top). By kind permission of Marquess of Tavistock and Trustees
of the Bedford Estate: page 17 (top). By permission of Viscount De
L'Isle, from his private collection: page 18. e.t. archive: pages 19,
28, 37 (bottom). The National Library of Scotland: page 20 (right),
reproduced with the permission of Sir Francis Ogilvy. Scottish
National Portrait Gallery: page 21. By courtesy of the Trustees of the
British Museum: pages 23 top, 37 bottom. The Marquess of
Salisbury/Hatfield House/Fotomas Index: page 27. The Mary Rose
Trust: page 33. The National Maritime Museum, London: pages 40,
41.The British Library: pages 8, 43 (bottom).
Cover: National Portrait Gallery, Mansell Collection, Michael Holford.
Design by Peter Bennett, artwork by Stephen Conlin.

Artwork: Stefan Chabluk: all maps. Mark Bergin: pages 28/29,
38/39, 40/41. James Field: pages 4, 8/9, 12/13, 18/19, 20/21,
26/27, 32/33, 42/43. Bill Donohoe: pages 5, 10/11, 14/15, 22/23.
John James: pages 1, 6/7, 16/17, 24/25, 30/31, 34/35, 36/37, 46.
Malcolm Smythe: page 45. Hayward Art: page 44.

CONTENTS

TIMECHART, ABOUT THIS BOOK   4
MAP OF BRITAIN   4

INTRODUCTION   5

HENRY VII BRINGS PEACE   6

Henry VIIth coins

HENRY VIII COMES TO
THE THRONE   8

Henry VIII's jousting helmet

HENRY VIII AND WOLSEY   10

Gates of Hampton Court Palace

HENRY AND HIS SIX WIVES   12

Execution block and axe

END OF THE MONASTERIES   14

Cathedral window

EDWARD VI AND MARY I   16

Sticks and pole for burning a heretic

THE YOUNG QUEEN
ELIZABETH   18

The queen hunting on horseback

ELIZABETH AND
MARY, QUEEN OF SCOTS   20

Mary, Queen of Scots coin

TOWNS, TRADE AND
TRANSPORT   22

Wooden barrels and cloth sacks

ELIZABETHAN CLOTHES   24

Woman in head- and neck-dress

TOWN AND COUNTRY LIFE   26

Huntsman and dogs

SHAKESPEARE AND THE
THEATRE   28

Portrait of William Shakespeare

HOUSES GREAT AND SMALL   30

Front of a town house

FOOD AND DRINK   32

Jugs and flagons for beer

EDUCATION AND SCIENCE   34

A copy book and pen

CRIME AND PUNISHMENT   36

Criminal in the stocks

EXPLORERS AND PIRATES   38

An Elizabethan ship

THE SPANISH ARMADA   40

A fireship ablaze

ELIZABETH'S LAST YEARS   42

The queen's seal on a map

FAMOUS PEOPLE OF TUDOR TIMES   44

ROYAL TUDORS FAMILY TREE   45

GLOSSARY – DEFINITIONS OF
IMPORTANT WORDS   46

PLACES TO VISIT   47

INDEX   47

The Tudor Period

During the Tudor period people made and built things similar to everyday objects of today. The photographs in this book are mostly of things which come from that time.

The illustrations in this book are based on historical evidence. They have been painted by artists who have used drawings and descriptions from Tudor times to help them to decide how things would have looked then.

ROMAN BRITAIN 55BC to AD406	SAXONS AND VIKINGS 406 to 1066	THE MIDDLE AGES 1066 to 1485	THE TUDORS 1485 to 1603	THE STUARTS 1603 to 1714	THE GEORGIANS 1714 to 1837	VICTORIAN BRITAIN 1837 to 1901	MODERN BRITAIN 1901 to the 1990s

ABOUT THIS BOOK

This book considers the Tudors chronologically, meaning that events are described in the order in which they happened, from 1485 to 1603. Most of the double-page articles deal with a particular part of Tudor history. Those that deal with aspects of everyday life such as trade, houses and clothing, are more general and cover the whole period. This is because these things did not change each time a new king or queen came to the throne. Unfamiliar words are explained in the glossary on page 46.

About the map

This shows the location of places mentioned in the text. Some are major cities, others towns or the sites of battles or famous buildings.

MAP OF BRITAIN

SHETLAND ISLANDS

FAIR ISLE

SCOTLAND

- Flodden
- Newcastle
- Rievaulx Abbey
- Lancaster
- York
- Halifax
- Manchester
- Liverpool

ULSTER

IRELAND

ENGLAND
- Louth
- Lincoln
- Walsingham
- Castle Acre
- Tutbury Castle
- Fotheringhay Castle
- Huntingdon
- Bosworth
- Kenilworth
- Lavenham
- Warwick Castle
- Stratford-on-Avon
- Northampton

WALES

- Oxford
- London
- Westminster
- Tower of London
- R. Thames
- Westminster Abbey
- Pembroke
- Tintern Abbey
- Hampton Court
- Bermondsey
- Canterbury
- Bristol
- Southwark Cathedral
- Gravelines
- Glastonbury Abbey
- Calais
- Southampton
- Plymouth

ISLE OF WIGHT

ENGLISH CHANNEL

FRANCE

INTRODUCTION

The age of the Tudors lasted for over 100 years, from 1485 to 1603. It was one of the most exciting times in British history. There was peace after many years of civil wars. There was the Reformation, in which the English Church broke away from the power of the Roman Catholic Church. There was a huge growth in trade, with British sailors opening up new sea routes to East and West. And there were many great writers, such as William Shakespeare, who produced some of the finest poetry and plays in the world.

The Tudor Age began on 22 August 1485. This was the date of the Battle of Bosworth. It was the last of the Wars of the Roses – the battles for the crown of England between the great families (called 'houses') of Lancaster and York. Richard III of York, the king at the time, was beaten by Henry Tudor, a Welshman from the House of Lancaster. In October, Henry was crowned as King Henry VII of England.

The Tudors ruled England and Wales, and also controlled a part of Ireland. Scotland was ruled by the Stuart family. There were four main classes of people. By far the biggest class was made up of labourers and poor people. Most of them lived in the countryside. Above them were the yeomen, who often worked small farms. Next were the merchants and master craftsmen of the towns. At the top were wealthy people and the nobles, who could have their own armies, and the leaders of the Church. Many of them spent their time at the monarch's court, and helped to govern the country in Parliament.

HENRY VII BRINGS PEACE

Henry became king by defeating Richard III at Bosworth in 1485. This ended the wars between the Lancastrians and the Yorkists. But Henry's claim to the throne was not very strong, and he had many enemies. Among these were the Yorkist followers of Richard III and other relatives of the previous king, Edward IV. In 1486, Henry married Elizabeth of York and so united both sides. He punished those who had fought for Richard III by taking away their lands.

Kings usually used Parliament to make laws and collect taxes. But Henry wanted to keep power in his own hands. So he governed through the King's Council. This was made up of about 200 noblemen, gentry and churchmen, whom he chose. The Council's real work was done by small courts and committees, closely controlled by Henry himself.

▷ **This portrait of Henry VII** was painted in 1505. He is holding a red rose, the symbol of the House of Lancaster. His reign brought lasting peace to England after almost 30 years of unrest. His marriage and the birth of his children made sure a Tudor would be the monarch for many years to come. His eldest son, Arthur, was to marry a Spanish princess, Catherine (Katerina) of Aragon, as a link between England and Spain. When Arthur died soon afterwards, special permission was given by the Pope, the Head of the Roman Catholic Church, for Catherine to marry Arthur's brother, Henry.

▽ **An important part of the King's Council was the Court of Star Chamber.** This is how we think it looked. The Court was a group of royal advisors which sat at Westminster. It often held trials of rich and powerful people who were accused of breaking the laws of the land.

△ **The Earl of Warwick** was a nephew of Edward IV, the Yorkist king who had died in 1483. He could be used by enemy nobles to take the crown from Henry. Henry had Warwick imprisoned in the Tower of London. He was let out once, and led through the streets to show he was still alive.

△ **In 1486, a boy named Lambert Simnel** pretended that he was the Earl of Warwick, and so the rightful king of England. Henry's enemies supported this 'pretender'. The rebel army was soon defeated by the king's forces, and Simnel was sent to work in the royal kitchens.

△ **Perkin Warbeck** was another 'pretender' to the English throne. He claimed to be a son of Edward IV, and tried several times to invade England from France with his troops. Warbeck was captured in 1497 and put in the Tower of London. He was executed in 1499, along with the Earl of Warwick.

Money was another big problem for Henry. After years of unrest and weak rule, the monarchy was very poor. Gradually, the king paid off his debts, and grew rich again. He made sure that every penny of tax was collected and paid to him. People who lived on his lands were charged higher rents. Anyone who broke the law had to pay large fines. Henry even forced rich people to lend him money.

The king appointed a number of special ministers to collect his taxes. These men were very unpopular, especially Edmund Dudley and Sir Richard Empson. Both were executed as soon as Henry VIII came to the throne.

HENRY VIII COMES TO THE THRONE

In 1515, a Venetian ambassador called Henry VIII "The handsomest monarch I ever set eyes upon: above the usual height…with a round face so very beautiful it would become a pretty woman".

Henry VIII was very different from his father. He was big and handsome and wore fine clothes. He loved playing in games, horse-riding and hunting. He spoke four languages, wrote poetry and played music. He seemed an ideal ruler.

▽ **This is one of the earliest known portraits of Henry VIII as king.** It was painted in 1518, when he was 27 years old. The picture shows him as handsome and still slim. Compare it with the portraits of Henry on pages 10 and 15.

△ **Musicians** playing for a dance during a party at Henry's court.

△ **The king composed** many pieces of music, including this song.

Henry wanted to be a strong king, with a firm hold on the throne. Above all, he wanted a son who would succeed him. In 1511 he was delighted when his wife, Queen Catherine, had a baby boy. But the son died soon afterwards. Catherine had five more children, but only one girl, Mary, survived. Meanwhile, Henry looked for glory by fighting wars. In 1513, he led an army to France to try and capture the French crown. Three weeks later, another of his armies defeated the Scots at Flodden. But his expeditions to France all failed, and he never gained control of Scotland. A lot of money and lives were wasted in these wars.

◁ **The king held a tournament** in London to celebrate the birth of his son. Henry took part in the jousting. His horse's covering bore the initials H for Henry, K for Catherine.

▽ **In 1520 a grand meeting** was arranged between Henry and Francis I, king of France, to make peace. It took place near Calais, and was called 'The Field of the Cloth of Gold' because of the rich materials used for the tents and decorations. The kings became friends, but three years later were at war again.

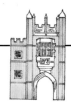

HENRY VIII AND WOLSEY

For the first half of his reign, Henry took little interest in the daily business of governing the country. He left this to his ministers. The most powerful of these was Thomas Wolsey, who was chief minister from 1514 to 1529.

◁ **Henry VIII looking proud**, as painted by Hans Holbein in the 1530s. Holbein was a German portrait artist who had settled in England in 1532.

△ **The Pope's gold seal** granting Henry the title 'Fidei Defensor', Defender of the Faith. Shortened to F.D., this still appears on British coins.

The king was left free to enjoy his sports and music. But he also had more serious hobbies, including the study of the Christian faith. England was still a Catholic country, and the English Church was ruled by the Pope in Rome. When a German called Martin Luther spoke badly of the Catholic Church, Henry wrote a book condemning him. For this, the Pope gave Henry the title Defender of the Faith, in 1521.

▷ **Wolsey grew very rich**, and used his wealth to build grand houses. Grandest of these was the palace at Hampton Court, on the River Thames. Here, Henry's royal barge sails towards Hampton Court.

Great Harry in full sail

◁ **Henry and Wolsey spent huge sums of money** on the army and navy. The most expensive project was the building of the warship *Great Harry*, which was launched in 1514. She was the biggest in the world. She had four masts, and gold-coloured sails for state occasions. There was a crew of 700 men, and she was armed with 21 bronze cannons. She was destroyed by accident in a fire on the Thames in 1553.

Wolsey was an ambitious man, and grew strong very quickly. By 1515 he was chief minister and Lord Chancellor, leader of the King's Council, chief judge in the law courts, Bishop of Lincoln and Archbishop of York. The Pope made him a cardinal, and his special ambassador. Wolsey had now become the most powerful person in England after the king. He controlled the law, the Church and managed the country's money.

▷ **Thomas Wolsey** in his cardinal's robes. He was vain and greedy, and loved to show off his wealth. This made him very unpopular. When he increased taxes, the people hated him even more. Wolsey's downfall came in 1529, when he was unable to persuade the Pope to give the king a divorce from Catherine.

Wolsey used his power to improve the courts and keep the nobles under control. Wealthy people were fined or imprisoned for keeping private armies. Landowners were stopped from building enclosures around their estates since these took land away from ordinary people. Wolsey also tried to make England more powerful in Europe. He helped Henry in his wars against France, and made treaties with other countries. But most of his plans failed through lack of money.

11

HENRY AND HIS SIX WIVES

In 1527, Catherine of Aragon was 42 years old. She could have no more children. The king still wanted a son to take the throne after him. He had also fallen in love with a young courtier named Anne Boleyn. He was determined to divorce Catherine and marry Anne.

There was one problem. Only the Pope, as head of the Church, could give permission to end the first marriage. Henry ordered Wolsey to arrange what was called 'the King's Great Matter'. But the Pope refused to allow the divorce.

Henry was furious. He blamed Wolsey, and dismissed him in 1529. He replaced him with Thomas More, a lawyer and scholar. But More was also a loyal Catholic, and thought the king was wrong to divorce Catherine. He resigned in 1532. The new chief minister was Thomas Cromwell, who was prepared to do what Henry wanted. Cromwell had a simple solution to the problem – the king must become head of the English Church.

△ **Catherine of Aragon** was a popular and faithful queen. But she had no sons, and the king tired of her. After 1525 they lived apart. Catherine never saw her daughter Mary again. She lived quietly until her death in 1536.

△ **Anne Boleyn** came to the English court in 1523. She soon attracted the king. Their marriage was brief, however. In 1533 she had a daughter, Elizabeth. Anne was beheaded in 1536 for being unfaithful to Henry.

◁ **Henry VIII and Anne Boleyn riding together.** They flirted openly. In 1532 the king made her Marquess of Pembroke. Soon afterwards, Anne became pregnant. The pair were secretly married in 1533. And as soon as Thomas Cranmer, the Archbishop of Canterbury, had ended the king's marriage with Catherine of Aragon, Anne was crowned as the new queen of England in Westminster Abbey.

There now began one of the biggest upheavals in English history. Henry and Cromwell broke the 1,000-year link with the Catholic Church in Rome. At first, they tried to change only the leader of the Church in England and not the religion itself. Between 1532 and 1534, Parliament made many rules that ended the Pope's power in England. The king became the Supreme Head of the Church of England. If Henry and Anne had any children, they would inherit the throne instead of Catherine's daughter. The king punished anyone who opposed him. When Thomas More refused to accept the new laws, he was executed.

△ **Jane Seymour** became the king's third wife in 1536, just 11 days after Anne's execution. Her son, Edward, was born in 1537. Jane herself died soon after. Henry probably loved her the best of all his wives.

△ **Anne of Cleves** was a German princess. Cromwell arranged for her to marry Henry in 1540, to make a link between England and Germany. But the king found her ugly, and they divorced six months later.

△ **Catherine Howard** was only 20 years old when she married Henry in July 1540. He was 49. Like Anne Boleyn, Catherine was unfaithful to the king. She was tried for treason, found guilty, and executed in 1542.

△ **Catherine Parr** became Henry's last wife in 1543. She liked family life, and brought the three royal children to live together at court for the first time. She looked after the young Elizabeth until her own death in 1548.

◁ **A painting of Henry VIII with Jane Seymour and his three children.** Edward and his mother sit on either side of Henry. Mary is on the far left. Elizabeth is on the right. These people could not have met at the ages they are shown. Henry had the picture painted to show clearly how the crown of England would pass from one member of his family to another. Edward was next to reign, from 1547 to 1553.

END OF THE MONASTERIES

"Level, level with the ground the towers do lie, which with their golden glittering tops pierced once to the sky!" – a song about the destruction of a shrine.

In 1535, Henry appointed Thomas Cromwell as his Vicar General. Cromwell made a survey of the 800 monasteries and nunneries in the land. It showed that many priests were rich, lazy and greedy.

At the time Henry became head of the English Church, priests were unpopular with both nobles and peasants. Henry decided to reform the Church and to take its wealth for himself. In 1536, Parliament passed an act 'dissolving', or getting rid of, the smaller monasteries. Another act in 1539 dissolved the larger ones.

Cromwell's men visited abbeys, priories and other religious houses. They sent the priests away, seized the money and other treasures, and destroyed the buildings. Riches poured into the king's coffers. But Henry soon started a costly new war with France in 1543. By 1547, he was bankrupt again.

▷ **How the monasteries were sacked:**
- lead and copper sheets were torn from the roofs
- statues were pulled down and smashed
- paintings were scratched or painted over
- ornaments were melted down for their gold or silver
- books from libraries were burned or sold
- stained glass windows were broken
- stones were taken away to build houses for the nobles and courtiers.

▷ **Holbein's portrait of Thomas Cromwell.**
A hard and loyal worker, Cromwell disliked the Catholic Church. He controlled Parliament for the king, creating the acts which established the Church of England and dissolved the monasteries. He also persuaded Henry to allow the Bible to be translated into English. In 1540 his enemies accused him of treason. He was executed.

▷ **Castle Acre Priory** in Norfolk is destroyed by Cromwell's officials in 1539. About 30 monks lived here. Many other fine church buildings were pulled down at this time, including Rievaulx Abbey in Yorkshire, Tintern Abbey in Gwent, and Glastonbury Abbey in Somerset.

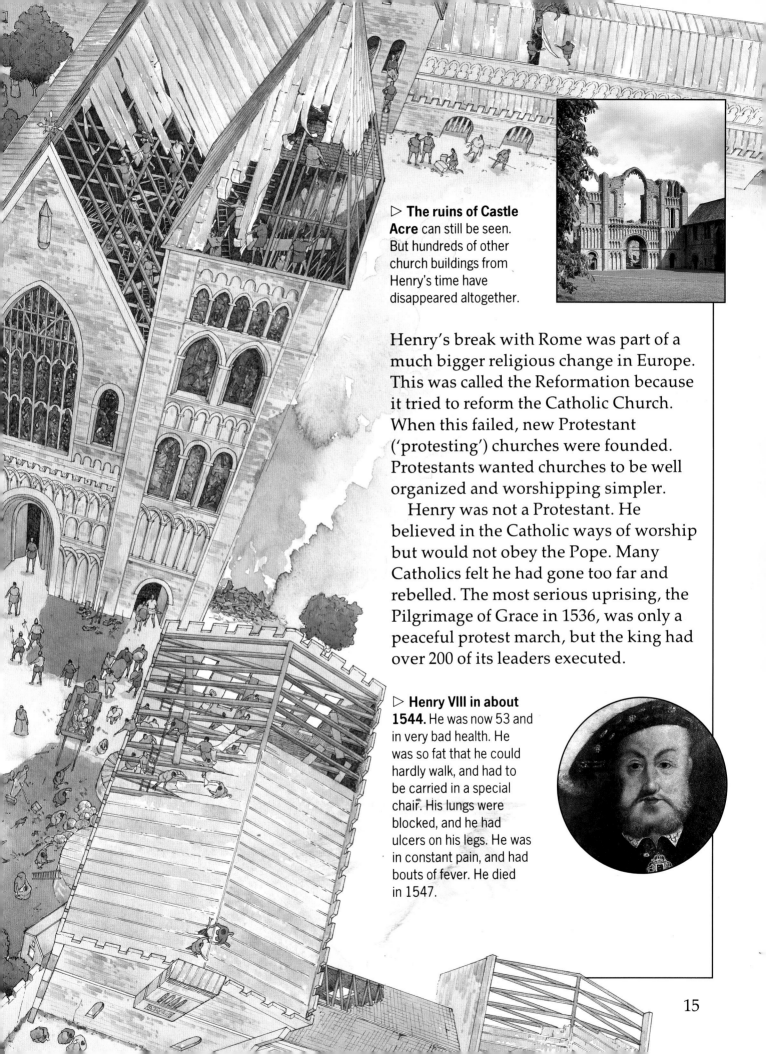

▷ **The ruins of Castle Acre** can still be seen. But hundreds of other church buildings from Henry's time have disappeared altogether.

Henry's break with Rome was part of a much bigger religious change in Europe. This was called the Reformation because it tried to reform the Catholic Church. When this failed, new Protestant ('protesting') churches were founded. Protestants wanted churches to be well organized and worshipping simpler.

Henry was not a Protestant. He believed in the Catholic ways of worship but would not obey the Pope. Many Catholics felt he had gone too far and rebelled. The most serious uprising, the Pilgrimage of Grace in 1536, was only a peaceful protest march, but the king had over 200 of its leaders executed.

▷ **Henry VIII in about 1544.** He was now 53 and in very bad health. He was so fat that he could hardly walk, and had to be carried in a special chair. His lungs were blocked, and he had ulcers on his legs. He was in constant pain, and had bouts of fever. He died in 1547.

15

EDWARD VI AND MARY I

Edward VI was only nine when he became king in 1547 so a 'Protector' governed for him. This was his uncle, the Duke of Somerset. In 1550, Somerset was replaced by the Duke of Northumberland.

Edward was a keen Protestant. During his reign, the new religion became firmly established in England. The first English Prayer Book was published by Archbishop Cranmer in 1549. The Bible had already been translated into English in the 1530s. Religious statues were banned. In 1552, Parliament passed an Act of Uniformity. This made it illegal to use any kind of religious service except the Protestant one.

▷ **The young king Edward.** During Edward's reign there were rebellions against religious changes, rising prices and lack of jobs. The uprisings showed Somerset to be a weak ruler, and led to his downfall in 1549.

▽ **Coronation** of Edward at Westminster Abbey.

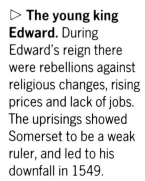

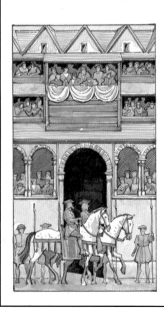

◁ **Two Protestant bishops, Hugh Latimer and Nicholas Ridley,** are about to be burned at the stake in Oxford in 1555.

△ **Mary and Philip after their wedding.** The prince went back to Spain a year later. He only returned for one visit.

△ **A page from the Book of Martyrs** of 1563 by John Foxe, a Protestant. The book contained stories about people burned by Mary.

Before Edward died of illness in 1553, he named 16-year-old Lady Jane Grey, Henry VII's great-granddaughter, as his successor. Edward did not want his Catholic sister Mary to become queen. However, Mary's claim to the throne was stronger. After just nine days as queen, Jane was imprisoned and beheaded. Mary wanted England to become a Roman Catholic country again. Leading Protestants, including Cranmer, were put in prison. Edward's new religious laws were scrapped. The queen made an alliance with Spain, a leading Catholic country. In 1554 she married Prince Philip, the heir to the Spanish throne. They had no children.

Mary also punished many heretics – people who refused to follow the religion of the country. The punishment was death, usually by burning. After 1555, Cranmer and 270 Protestant priests and ordinary people were burned at the stake. Their executions made Mary very unpopular. But she died in 1558.

THE YOUNG QUEEN ELIZABETH

Like Henry VIII, Elizabeth I was fond of getting her own way. And like Henry VII, she was thrifty and cautious. People said women made bad rulers, but Elizabeth disagreed. She once said, "Though I be a woman, I have as good a courage as my father had".

In 1558, England needed a strong and steady ruler after the violent changes of the Reformation and Mary's reign. The new queen chose a small council of trusted advisors. Among them was William Cecil, who served Elizabeth until he died in 1598.

First, the queen tried to settle the unrest over religion. In 1559, Parliament declared her to be 'Supreme Governor' of the Church, instead of 'Supreme Head'. She hoped this would please the Catholics. To please the Protestants, Elizabeth made all the churches use Cranmer's Prayer Book.

▷ **The queen dancing with Sir Robert Dudley.** He was her favourite courtier at the start of her reign. Although Elizabeth was not interested in marriage, she flirted with princes from Spain, France and Sweden to keep their countries on England's side.

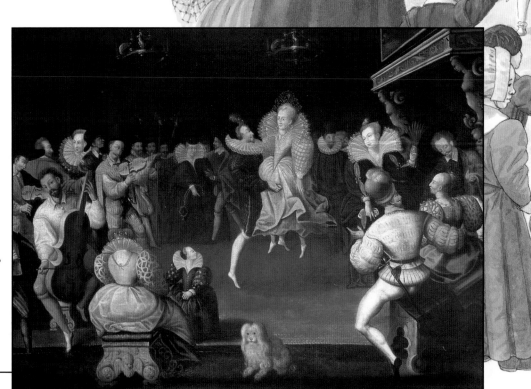

The queen's signature

18

◁ **Elizabeth loved to hunt deer**, as shown in this Tudor drawing. She was a very good rider. She wore fine clothes and jewels on horseback, but still rode faster than most of her companions. The courtiers who arranged the hunts for the queen also put on for her special plays and firework displays.

◁ **Elizabeth arrives at Hengrave Hall**, Suffolk, on a royal progress. She has taken with her:
● a litter, carried by servants (she sometimes rode, or went by carriage)
● her personal staff of maids, grooms and cooks
● a huge amount of her belongings, including clothes, jewellery and furniture
● as many as 400 wagons to carry it all
● 2,400 horses to pull the wagons
● bottles of her favourite beer
● at least 1,000 other servants and ministers.

The monarchy was poor in 1558. Elizabeth spent as little as possible by trying to stay out of costly foreign wars. She made peace with France in 1564, and did not fight Spain openly until 1585.

At home, the queen avoided large expenses. She built no great palaces and kept fewer servants than the other Tudors. She also made money by selling royal lands and 'monopolies'. The buyer of a monopoly was the only person allowed to make or sell certain goods. There were monopolies for wine, salt, coal and many other things.

In summer, Elizabeth and her household usually left London to stay with rich courtiers. This also saved money. The courtier had to provide entertainment and food. The tours, or 'progresses', also gave ordinary people the chance to see their ruler and even to speak with her.

ELIZABETH AND MARY, QUEEN OF SCOTS

Elizabeth had a rival for the throne. This was her beautiful Catholic cousin, Mary Stuart. Mary was already Queen of Scotland. Many Catholics believed she should be Queen of England as well.

Born in 1542, Mary had become Scottish queen as a baby when James V had died. Because of war between Scotland and England, she spent her childhood in France. There she married Francis, the French heir. But he died in 1560. In 1561 Mary returned to Scotland.

The Protestant faith had taken a firm hold in Scotland, and many Scots did not want a Catholic queen. In 1565, Mary married her cousin, Henry, Lord Darnley, but soon hated his bullying ways. Darnley was killed in a mysterious explosion. Many people blamed Mary and her friend Lord Bothwell for the murder. In 1567, Bothwell became Mary's third husband. The Scots rose in rebellion. Mary fled to England.

▷ **Sir Francis Walsingham** was head of Elizabeth's secret service. He had more than 70 spies in towns and ports throughout Europe. They sent him news of Catholic plots against the queen.

▷ **Mary Stuart with Lord Darnley, Duke of Albany**, in 1566. He was a weak and stupid person, and Mary spent most time with her secretary, David Riccio, instead.

◁ **Elizabeth and her Parliament.** The members were worried that Elizabeth had no children; Mary could claim the throne when Elizabeth died. From 1571, they urged her to act against Mary.

Mary landed in Cumbria in 1568. At once, she became the centre of attempts to kill Elizabeth. English Catholics, supported by France and Spain, wanted Mary to be queen.

Elizabeth knew that Mary was a threat. She also saw the danger of putting a queen on trial for plotting against her. But if she sent Mary abroad, Mary could then plot openly. She decided to keep her alive and imprisoned in England. In 1586, Walsingham found a letter from Mary approving a Catholic plot. She was found guilty of treason and executed.

▷ **Mary Stuart was held hostage at Tutbury Castle** in Staffordshire. She could send letters and have visitors, but Walsingham had her watched.

◁ **Mary was beheaded** in the great hall of Fotheringhay Castle near Northampton, in February 1587. She was plump and lame, and wore a red wig. One of her little dogs had hidden in her skirts.

Mary's death angered Catholics, especially the Spanish king. He used it as an excuse to plan war against England. Mary had left an heir. He became King James I.

TOWNS, TRADE AND TRANSPORT

By the 1560s, trade was booming in Europe. Many countries became rich. The Portuguese brought spices from the East, and the Spanish gold and silver from America. New machines, such as the spinning wheel, meant that more goods could be made and sold.

England became a major trading centre. Cloth from London went to Holland and France by boat. Ships from Bristol brought back fish from Newfoundland. Iron, salt, sugar, coal and wools were exported. As the great Dutch port of Antwerp declined, much of its business came to London. Bristol, Liverpool and other sea ports grew quickly. So did new centres of the cloth industry, such as Manchester and Halifax. But by far the biggest town was London.

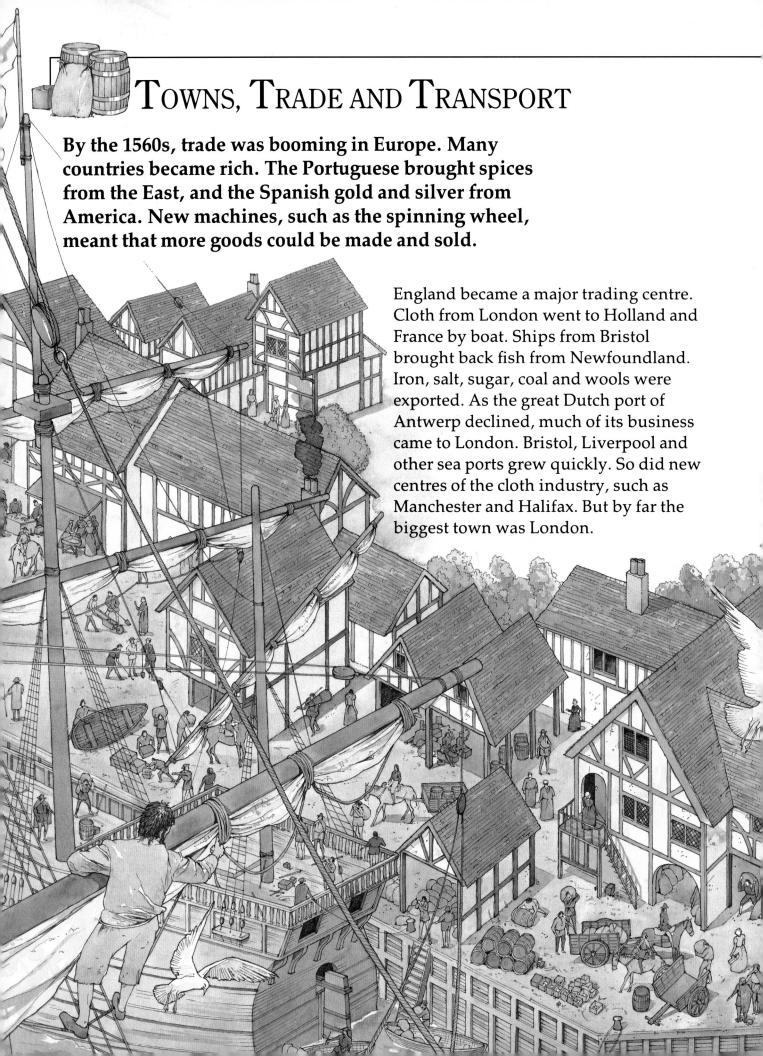

A group of about 800 London merchants controlled most of England's trade abroad. The merchants grew rich by buying goods from all over England and then selling them at a higher price to foreign traders. Some merchants formed companies to trade with special areas overseas. The Russia Company, founded in 1553, took cargo to the Russian port of Archangel. Other companies travelled south to Morocco and the Near East.

▽ **This print shows a wool merchant** in his warehouse. He is counting his money using a simple calculator called an abacus. The sphere above his head shows that his goods come from the countryside. Outside, his workers pack the wool in sacks and tie the tops. Wool had been a major product for 300 years.

Tudor coins

◁ **Some of the goods which might come to this port:**
- coal from Newcastle
- copper from Cumbria
- lead from Somerset
- tin from Cornwall
- cast iron from Kent
- wire from Gwent
- woollen cloth from Norfolk and Lancashire
- sugar from London
- salt from Scotland
- cod from Iceland and Newfoundland
- wine from France
- olive oil from Spain
- furs from Russia.

▽ **A carrier** with his covered wagon. Carriers took goods to sell from town to town. Some took passengers as well.

◁ **A bustling sea port in the 1570s.** The dockers unload its ships and store the goods in the warehouse. From here the merchants sold the goods to other traders from towns inland.

Travelling across England was difficult and dangerous. Most roads were just muddy tracks, full of ruts and holes. There were few bridges, and most travellers had to cross rivers at shallow fords. Traders rode in groups to discourage robbers.

Most people travelled by horse. This was much faster and more comfortable than the early coaches, which had no springs to soften the bumps. Goods were carried by wagon or by groups of packhorses, and letters by couriers.

ELIZABETHAN CLOTHES

Young gentleman

"I like silk stockings well. Henceforth I will wear no more cloth stockings" – said by Elizabeth I in 1560.

The queen loved fine clothes. At the end of her life, she had 260 gowns, 99 robes, 127 cloaks, 125 petticoats and hundreds more pieces of finery in her wardrobe.

Wealthy Elizabethan women wore a lot of clothes each day. First came a thick smock and petticoat. Over these went a bodice and skirt. The skirt was held up by hoops and padded at the hips into what was called a bumrawle. An outer bodice and skirt covered this, and on top was a gown, which stretched to the floor.

Wealthy men wore a linen shirt and tight-fitting jacket called a doublet. Over these was another jacket, a jerkin, which came out over the hips. They wore stockings, and padded breeches instead of trousers. Most wore a velvet or fur hat.

▷ **A maid helps her mistress to get dressed.**
Besides clothes, women and men wore many 'extras'. There were separate sleeves and cuffs. 'Stomachers' were tied over the stomach to keep it flat, and starched ruffs worn around the neck. Fashions changed quickly. At one time, ruffs were so large that the wearer had to eat with a long-handled spoon.

▷ **Working clothes** started to look like uniforms – the butcher with his apron, the baker with his cap and loose clothing, the weaver's long dress and white cap, and the soldier with his jacket and helmet.

Butcher

Baker

Weaver

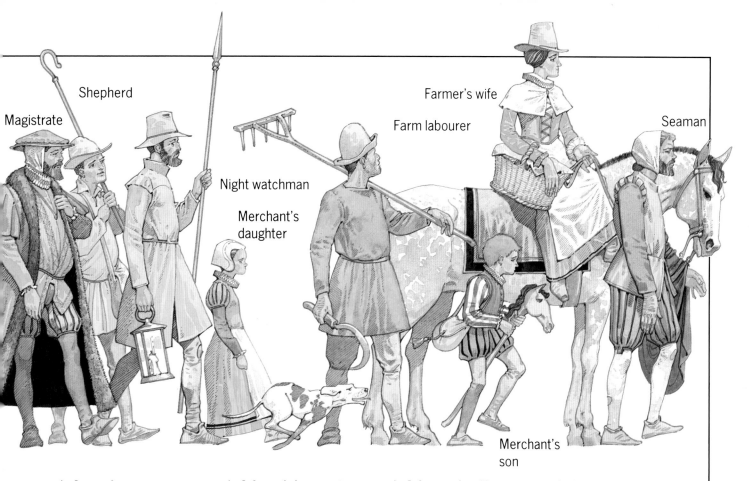

Magistrate · Shepherd · Night watchman · Merchant's daughter · Farmer's wife · Farm labourer · Seaman · Merchant's son

△ **A magistrate** wears a doublet with sleeves, wide breeches, and a gown edged with fur. He has a flat felt hat and stockings on his legs.

△ **A farm labourer** is dressed in a felt hat and homespun cloth tunic and breeches. His belt and shoes are made of thick leather.

△ **A farmer's wife** wears a big white apron over her plain gown and knitted stockings. Her straw hat has a wide brim to shade her face.

△ **A seaman** is dressed in a canvas jacket and long breeches. He carries a blue coat given to all sailors who fought against the Armada.

The finest clothes were made of linen, silk or the best wool cloth. But these were no use to farm labourers and other working folk. They were uncomfortable and too tight. Besides, few could afford to buy them. Most people earned less than £10 in a whole year, and a single silk gown might cost more than £80.

Workers wore loose-fitting tunics and shirts made of coarse woollen cloth. This was woven locally, and dyed brown or blue with vegetable dyes.

In 1571, a law was passed which forced everyone over the age of seven to wear a woollen cap on Sundays. This made more work for cap-makers and wool traders.

Soldier

◁ **Rich and poor.** This illustration from Tudor times compares the clothing of a wealthy landowner and a beggar. The poor, sick, orphans and people out of work were mostly given clothes by others.

TOWN AND COUNTRY LIFE

Most Elizabethans lived in the countryside. Only about one-fifth of the population lived in towns. Although the cities were growing fast, much of the land was still wild and lonely. There were deer, wild pigs and even wolves in parts of Wales and the North.

▽ **An illustration from a Tudor calendar** for February, showing a shepherd, a cattleman and a woman chopping down a tree.

Village life had changed little since the Middle Ages. Most villagers worked for the owner of the land around the village. They rented patches of ground from him to grow their crops. Their few cows, pigs and poultry grazed on common land. In good years, they could feed themselves and have food left over to sell at market. In bad years, they went hungry.

Few people went far from their village. Most of the tools, clothes and toys were made by local craftsmen such as the smith or the weaver. The only strangers they saw were the wandering friars, or pedlars from the towns selling goods.

▽ **Villages** had houses with gardens, small cottages, a church, and shared fields. Here, some villagers practise dancing around a maypole, some are at work, while others, who have crossed the bridge, go hunting.

▷ **How a village might have looked in Queen Elizabeth's day.** Can you see
- the riverside watermill, used for sawing timber
- the windmill, used for grinding flour
- the manor house, with its formal gardens
- the archery field, where villagers practised
- the shepherd tending his flock of sheep
- the church
- the villagers' fields by the bridge, divided into strips
- the farmer's fields, 'enclosed' by fences?

△ **This painting shows a marriage feast** at Bermondsey in about 1570. In the background you can see the River Thames and the Tower of London. Though the setting is near London, it looks like the country. Everyone is dressed in their finest clothes. Some guests are dancing.

▷ **There was plenty of entertainment** in an Elizabethan town. Many people liked cruel sports such as bear-baiting or cock-fighting (the building in the background is a cockpit). There were also many ale-houses. The children played ball games such as football, or spun tops and hoops.

Tudor villagers used trees to provide wood to make ships, houses, furniture and to burn for fires or to make charcoal. Charcoal was used as a fuel for smiths' furnaces.

Town centres were crowded and busy. The houses were mostly wooden, and built very close together. Fires were a great danger, and there were only leather or wooden water buckets for putting them out. It was easier to knock houses down to stop fires spreading.

Towns had no proper drains either. Dirty water and other rubbish was thrown into rivers, or into the streets. The only clean (or nearly clean) water was sold by water-carriers. There were many outbreaks of disease. Rich people preferred to live just outside the towns. There was more room for big houses with gardens. And the air was cleaner.

SHAKESPEARE AND THE THEATRE

When Elizabethans wanted excitement and entertainment, they went to the theatre. Every week, thousands of Londoners flocked to the new theatres around the city. Rich and poor alike were thrilled to see comedies and tragedies by the finest writers of the age. The greatest of these was William Shakespeare.

For centuries, actors had been despised as beggars or tramps. But in 1572 a new law forced all bands of actors to hold a special licence. As a result, they had to become better organized and more skilful. They soon gained respect as well. Many new acting companies were formed, usually supported by rich and powerful patrons. One of the most famous of these was called the Lord Chamberlain's Men. Shakespeare joined them in about 1594, working as an actor and writer.

▷ **A play at the Swan Theatre**, built in 1595.

◁ **Christopher Marlowe** was Shakespeare's closest rival as a poet and playwright. Among his plays were *Doctor Faustus* and *Tamburlaine*. He was killed in a tavern brawl at the age of 29.

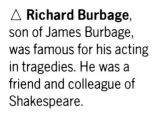

△ **Richard Burbage**, son of James Burbage, was famous for his acting in tragedies. He was a friend and colleague of Shakespeare.

▷ **The Globe Theatre** was constructed on Bankside in Southwark, south London. This was an area of theatres, bear-baiting rings, taverns and inns.

◁ **Dramatist and poet William Shakespeare** is still the world's most famous writer. He completed at least 37 plays, most of which were hugely popular. Although he wrote mostly in verse, he used everyday language that the Elizabethans could easily understand. His greatest plays include the tragedies *Hamlet* and *Macbeth*, and the comedies *Twelfth Night* and *A Midsummer Night's Dream*.

Shakespeare was born in Stratford-on-Avon, where you can see his house and the house of his wife, Anne Hathaway.

At first, the wandering companies performed their plays in the streets or the courtyards of inns. Then in 1576 an actor called James Burbage built England's first public theatre, in north London. Shakespeare's company acted at the Globe Theatre, built in 1599.

The theatre surrounded an open courtyard. The richer members of the audience sat on benches in the galleries, which were sheltered from the weather. The rest crowded into the yard, or pit. They were called the 'groundlings'.

The stage was a platform that jutted out into the pit. The audience watched the action from the front or the sides. The actors entered and left the stage through doorways at the back. There were about 12 men and boys in each company, but no women. The female roles were taken by boys.

HOUSES GREAT AND SMALL

The Tudors built many thousands of new houses. A few were grand palaces made of stone, but most were smaller, 'half-timbered' town houses or simple country cottages. They had wooden frames pinned together with wooden pegs, and the spaces filled with clay or brick.

The builders used local materials for the wall fillings. In Norfolk, the clay was mixed with flint, and in Devon, with gravel and straw. In Essex, the timber frame was covered with wooden boards. Walls were often plastered over outside.

▷ **This Tudor town house** has a narrow front facing the street. Below it is a cellar for storage. The ground floor has a workshop with a kitchen behind it. On the first floor is the big main family living room, which juts out over the street. Above this is the garret, or attic, where the servants slept. The roof is covered in clay tiles. The chimneystack is made of brick. The timbers have been weather-proofed.

▽ **Burghley House** in Northamptonshire is a fine example of a grand Tudor house. It was built in 1589 by William Cecil, Lord Burghley, who was Elizabeth I's main advisor.

△ **Farmhouses were built of stone,** gathered from nearby fields and quarries. This one, next to a barn, is only one room wide. There are two rooms on the lower floor. Upstairs is the sleeping area for the whole family. The chimney is half-timbered, which is a fire hazard, and there is no glass in the windows.

Houses in Tudor times were more comfortable than ever before. Instead of holes in the roof to let out smoke, they had proper chimneys. This made the rooms warmer, and stopped a thatched roof from catching fire. Many houses had glass windows. Glass was expensive but gave more light than old-fashioned horn or wooden shutters.

Many palaces had marble floors while farmhouses had floors of stone. Cottage floors were usually just beaten earth. Only the rich could afford carpets, so most people covered their floors with rushes, reeds or straw mixed with sweet-smelling herbs. These were changed every month.

◁ **Almost all the furniture inside this house** is made of wood. Only important people, such as the master or mistress of the house, had chairs. The rest sat on benches or stools. Beds consisted of feather mattresses covered with thick sheets and wool blankets. The walls had wood panelling to keep out draughts.

FOOD AND DRINK

Most Elizabethans ate very well. The main part of each meal was meat. Besides beef, lamb, pork and poultry, there was rabbit, deer, goat and wildfowl. Rich people even ate swans. Everyone, by law, had to eat fish, not meat, on Fridays and during Lent.

Until the 1580s, vegetables and fruit were less popular. By the end of the century there were many more vegetable and fruit gardens, and many new varieties were available, but only for the rich. From Europe came raspberries and gooseberries. And from America came peppers, pumpkins and potatoes.

▽ **Cooking a meal** in a town worker's house. Ordinary people lived, cooked, ate and slept in the same room. Here, meat is being boiled in a pot over an open fire. It will be eaten with bread and beer or cider.

How rich and poor ate:
● *Bread* The rich ate bread made of white or wholemeal flour: poor people's bread was made of rye or ground acorns.
● *Butter and eggs* Rich people regarded them as food for the poor.
● *Sugar* This came from Asia and was expensive and hard to get. Honey was more usually used to sweeten food.
● *Drink* The rich drank wine from France and Spain; other people drank ale, cider or buttermilk.

△ **Countrywomen** make their way to market to sell their goods. Two of them have set up a stall to sell fish caught that morning.

▷ **Farmers** had very little winter feed for their animals, so most cattle and pigs were killed in the autumn. Some of the meat was preserved; the rest had to be eaten quickly.

◁ **To preserve meat,** farmers covered it in salt and packed it in wooden barrels. Spices and sauces made from herbs were used to mask any rotten taste.

△ **Plates, spoons, jug and tankard** found in the wreck of the Tudor ship, *Mary Rose*. Many people had pewter plates and cups, although the rich ate from silver plates and drank from wine glasses. Knives and spoons were used, but forks were still rare.

Feasts and banquets took place in the great hall of a big house. The host and important guests sat at the head table, which was raised on a platform. The rest sat lower down. There was usually a vast amount of food. The dishes were set out on side tables, and the guests chose what they wanted. Glasses and cups also stood at the side. The diner drank, then handed the cup back to a servant, who wiped it and put it aside. This stopped people from drinking too much.

Often, there was a lot of food left over. This was given to the servants. Anything they did not eat was given to beggars who waited outside the kitchen door.

Herbs and spices

Beers and wines

▽ **The kitchen of a grand house.** There are wood fires for cooking meat, which is held above the flames on turning spits. Bread is baked in a special brick oven. In the centre is a large table for preparing the food. Beneath the table are stored barrels of water and wine.

▷ **Dishes of prepared foods** are carried to the great hall. This is a long way from the kitchen, and the food may be cold when it gets there!

Most Tudor households brewed their own beer, both strong and 'small' (weak). In fruit-growing areas, cider (from apples) and perry (from pears) was made. Besides these, Elizabethans drank nearly 30,000 barrels of foreign wine each year.

EDUCATION AND SCIENCE

Schools were mainly for rich children. Before the Reformation of the 1540s, most schools were run by the Church, with the priests as teachers. These were shut as the monasteries closed. In their place came grammar schools, founded by wealthy merchants. Most pupils were boys; few girls were educated.

▷ **A Latin lesson** in an Elizabethan grammar school. Only rich boys went to these schools. In wealthy families, girls may have been taught at home by a tutor. Their mothers taught them how to run a household.

△ **A horn book,** used by Tudor schoolchildren. It was a flat board with a handle. On it was a sheet of paper with the alphabet or the Lord's Prayer. This was often protected by a thin piece of clear animal horn.

△ **The seal** of Louth Grammar School in 1552. It shows a teacher beating a pupil with his whip. The words mean "Spare the rod and spoil the child".

Pupils spent a long time at school. After three years at a 'petty' or nursery school, they went to a grammar school at the age of seven. There were only two holidays, of about two weeks each, at Christmas and Easter. During the rest of the year, only Sundays and saints' days were free.

The school day began at 6 or 7 o'clock in the morning. The most important subjects were Latin and Divinity. The boys had to learn long passages by heart. They would usually be beaten if they forgot anything. Lunch was at 11 o'clock, and afternoon lessons lasted from 1 o'clock until 5. On fine days, pupils might be allowed outside to swim or practise archery.

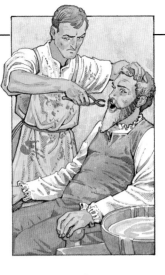

△ **A printer** at his press. Printing started in England in 1476. By the 1550s, copies of the Bible, the Prayer Book and many other books could be read in English for the first time.

△ **A barber surgeon** at work. These doctors did many jobs, from treating bullet wounds to pulling out rotten teeth. They also treated patients by cutting open veins to bleed them.

△ **John Dee** was a scientist who tried to turn ordinary metal into gold. He claimed to foretell the future by looking at the stars. Elizabeth I let him choose her coronation day, 15 January 1559.

△ **William Gilbert** was the queen's doctor. He also made early experiments with electricity. He believed that the Earth was a huge magnet – an idea later shown to be correct.

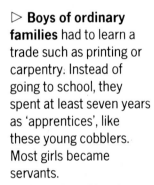

▷ **Boys of ordinary families** had to learn a trade such as printing or carpentry. Instead of going to school, they spent at least seven years as 'apprentices', like these young cobblers. Most girls became servants.

◁ **A glass bottle-maker's workshop.**

A—BLOW-PIPE. B—LITTLE WINDOW. C—MARBLE. D—FORCEPS. E—MOULDS BY MEANS OF WHICH THE SHAPES ARE PRODUCED.

New ideas and machines helped industry to grow rapidly. Coal mines were drained of water with pumps, driven by horses, so they could be worked safely. Coal became the main fuel in the making of glass, bricks and, later, iron. Copper was also mined, and made into brass for guns. At the same time, more gunpowder was produced. Now England had her own guns and explosives to use in war.

CRIME AND PUNISHMENT

In Tudor times, there were hundreds of murders and robberies every year, and the constant threat of rebellion. The monarchs made harsh laws to keep the peace, but they had no police force or permanent army to help them. They relied on local constables and on the Justices of the Peace.

There were about 700 Justices, or JPs, in Elizabethan England and Wales. They were not paid, but had many jobs to do. They made sure people went to church. They settled arguments between masters and servants. They ordered rioters to go home. And, of course, they tried people accused of crimes in the local courts.

▽ **Two JPs sit in court.** A vagrant has been brought before them by the local watchmen. The JP on the right holds a 'clearance order'. This commands the vagrant to leave the district and go back to his own parish. Note the scented pomander on the bench to mask the man's smell.

As England's population rose, there were fewer jobs. Many people were out of work. Peasants were forced from their villages by landlords who turned their fields and common lands into sheep pasture. By 1570 there were more than 10,000 homeless people wandering the roads, looking for work and begging. This became serious. In 1547, a law was made ordering vagrants to be whipped and sent to their home towns. This stopped one town having to pay to help the poor of another town.

The law was just as harsh on others. In the 1580s, many women were hanged for witchcraft. Dishonest shopkeepers were chained into stocks, where they would be pelted with rubbish by local people.

A witch is dunked in a river as a punishment.

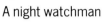

Whipping a vagrant

A night watchman

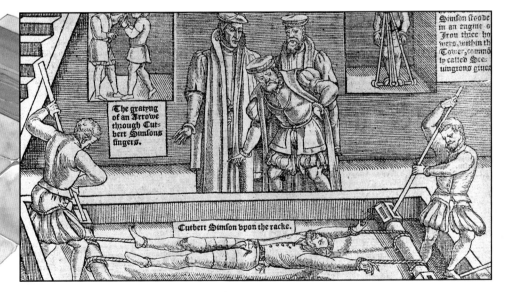

△ **A night watchman** patrols the streets with his dog and his lantern. Merchants hired private watchmen to guard their warehouses at night. The other lawkeepers were the constables, or 'beadles'. They organized groups to chase robbers and rioters.

△ **A Protestant rebel**, Cuthbert Simson, is subjected to various tortures in the Tower of London in 1558, including being stretched on a rack. He was punished by Catholic Mary I, whose ministers look on.

◁ **A criminal is hanged** in a city square. People could be hanged for minor crimes such as forging and stealing coins. In 1598, 74 people were hanged in Devon alone. Only noblemen or the gentry were beheaded.

△ **Tudor coins with their edges cut off** by forgers. The metal clippings were melted down and made into 'forged' coins.

Explorers And Pirates

By 1521, Spanish and Portuguese explorers had found sea routes to America and the Pacific. English sailors soon followed them. They were in search of new trading links, new lands to settle – and the treasure carried in Spanish ships.

Most Elizabethan ships were less than 40 metres long, and had three or four masts. They were heavy and hence slow and hard to steer, and they rolled in high seas.

Beneath the main deck was the gun deck, where the cannons were fixed. Most of the crew slept in this crowded space. The captain and senior officers had separate cabins. The sailors' main food was salt meat, peas and bread.

▽ **The trade routes to America and voyages of exploration** in Elizabethan times. Slaves were shipped from West Africa to the Caribbean where they were sold to the Spanish settlers in return for sugar, ginger, animal skins (hides) and pearls.

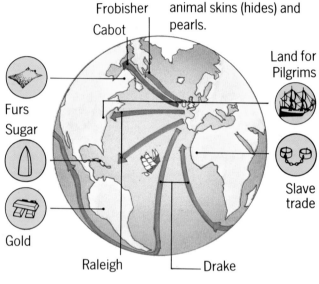

Frobisher
Cabot
Furs
Sugar
Gold
Land for Pilgrims
Slave trade
Raleigh
Drake

▽ **English settlers** on Roanoke Island off Virginia, North America, in 1584. A colony was founded here by Walter Raleigh. More settlers came in 1585. But because of little support from England, the settlers abandoned it.

Elizabethan warship

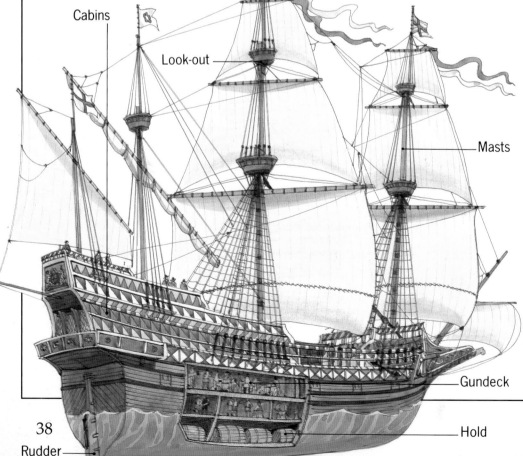

Cabins
Look-out
Masts
Gundeck
Hold

38
Rudder

▷ **Sir Walter Raleigh and his son Wat.** Raleigh was a soldier and poet, and one of Elizabeth I's favourites. After the Roanoke colony failed, he set out in 1595 for Guiana in South America. He was looking for El Dorado, the fabled city of gold, but found nothing. After Elizabeth died, Raleigh was distrusted by James I, who put him in prison. In 1617 the king gave him a last chance to find El Dorado. It too failed, and Raleigh was executed.

Tudor Explorers
1497 John Cabot reaches Nova Scotia, North America.
1508 Sebastian Cabot sails into Hudson Bay, North America.
1527 Cabot explores the coast of Paraguay, South America.
1553 Willoughby and Chancellor sail to Russia.
1576 Frobisher explores the Hudson Strait.
1580 Drake completes his voyage round the world.
1595 Raleigh sails to Guiana, South America.
1601 Lancaster sets up a trading base on Java in the Indian Ocean.

The Spanish had conquered much of South and Central America by 1550. Their fleets carried back to Europe a vast wealth of gold and silver. Although Spain and England were not openly at war, they were already enemies. So the queen did not stop privateers such as John Hawkins from attacking the treasure ships.

The most famous of all privateers was Sir Francis Drake. In 1572, he raided Spanish ports in the West Indies and Panama. In 1577, he set out on his voyage round the world. With three ships, Drake sailed up the Pacific coast of South America, capturing a huge amount of gold and silver. He returned home in 1580 to be knighted.

The Spanish gathered a fleet in Cadiz harbour in 1587, ready to invade England. Drake sailed into the harbour and destroyed over 20 of the Spanish warships. This delayed the sailing of the Spanish fleet. Drake called it "the singeing of the King of Spain's beard".

▷ **An English privateer** closes in on a Spanish treasure ship. Big and slow, these galleons were easy to catch. Once on board, the attackers would force the crew to surrender. The treasure ship would then be sailed back to England.

THE SPANISH ARMADA

In 1587 King Philip II of Spain drew up plans for war against Queen Elizabeth. A huge fleet, or armada, of 130 ships would sail up the English Channel to the Netherlands. There it would join an army of 30,000 men and take them to the English coast. The invaders would capture the southern ports and march on London. The English Catholics would rise in rebellion to drive Elizabeth from the throne.

The Armada left Lisbon in May 1588, but soon ran into a storm and supplies were lost. The Spanish admiral, the Duke of Medina Sidonia, already feared the worst.

The English fleet, led by Lord Howard and Sir Francis Drake, attacked the Armada on 21 July near Plymouth. Medina Sidonia tried to escape but knew he was trapped. He ordered his fleet to drop anchor near Calais harbour.

▽ **The Armada portrait of Queen Elizabeth.** The background scenes show, on the left, the English fleet and fireships about to attack Spanish ships and, on the right, the Armada in a gale. Elizabeth has her right hand on a globe, to show that England ruled the seas.

△ **English sailors** unroll their ship's sails to sail among and fire guns at the Spanish Armada. But they could not break the Armada's tight formation.

△ **Lord Howard and Sir Francis Drake.** Drake was known to the Spaniards as El Draco, meaning the dragon, since he attacked Spanish ports in America and stole their gold for Queen Elizabeth.

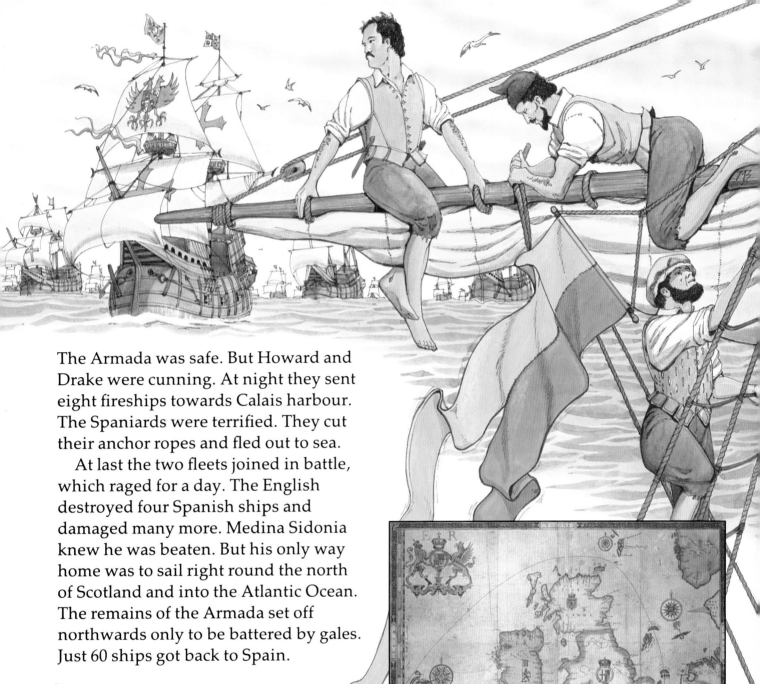

The Armada was safe. But Howard and Drake were cunning. At night they sent eight fireships towards Calais harbour. The Spaniards were terrified. They cut their anchor ropes and fled out to sea.

At last the two fleets joined in battle, which raged for a day. The English destroyed four Spanish ships and damaged many more. Medina Sidonia knew he was beaten. But his only way home was to sail right round the north of Scotland and into the Atlantic Ocean. The remains of the Armada set off northwards only to be battered by gales. Just 60 ships got back to Spain.

△ **Medina Sidonia** led the Armada in the *San Martin de Portugal*. He was one of the survivors who got back to Spain.

△ **The Spanish guns** were powerful but had a short range. The English guns shot further but were not accurate.

△ **The route taken by the Armada** is shown on this map, made some years later. The fleet assembled at Lisbon in Portugal then set sail for the English Channel. After the ships cut their anchor ropes at Calais and fled out to sea, they were met by the English fleet off Gravelines, on the Flemish coast. They then sailed northwards as far as the Fair Isle, before heading south. They sailed round the west coast of Ireland and headed due south back to Spain.

ELIZABETH'S LAST YEARS

The queen was 60 years old in 1594. She was still full of energy, and rode, hunted and danced. She was also able to terrify ministers and courtiers.

"Though God hath raised me high, yet this I count the glory of my crown, that I have reigned with your loves". So said Elizabeth I to Parliament in 1601.

Elizabeth's last years were full of troubles. The war with Spain was costly. Her trusted chief minister, Burghley, died in 1598. Because she had never married, there was no heir to follow her, and she refused to choose who would be the next monarch. Yet she still wanted to impress friends and enemies.

▽ **The queen is dressed by her ladies.** As she grew older, she grew more vain. She wore a red wig to cover her grey hair, and a thick layer of make-up to hide her wrinkles. She was dressed in fine robes and many jewels. She liked sweet food, and many of her teeth were black from rot or were missing.

◁ **Only one artist** could paint the queen from life, but all portraits had to flatter her. Ones she did not like were burned.

▷ **A portrait of Robert Devereux**, the 2nd Earl of Essex, in about 1585. His wit and good looks attracted Elizabeth, who gave him many honours. But he disobeyed her several times. In 1589 he joined Francis Drake on an expedition to Portugal against her wishes.

The ageing queen had one last favourite. This was her cousin, the 2nd Earl of Essex. He was a brave soldier, and Elizabeth gave him command of an expedition to France in 1591. This was a disaster, but the queen forgave him.

In 1599, Essex led an army to overcome a rebellion in Ireland. He disobeyed his orders and made peace with the rebel leader. Then he returned home without permission. Elizabeth was furious, and imprisoned him for a year.

Essex was vain and ambitious. He wanted to rule the country, and decided to overthrow the queen. In 1601, he rode into London and tried to start a revolt. But he was soon captured, then tried for treason, and beheaded.

▷ **Part of the life-like marble tomb** of Elizabeth I, which can be seen in the Henry VII Chapel at Westminster Abbey.

Queen Elizabeth died on 24 March 1603. During her long reign, England had become a strong country in Europe. There had been no civil wars, in spite of the unrest caused by the Reformation and by poverty. She named King James of Scotland, Mary's son, as her heir.

▽ **The queen's funeral procession** on its way to Westminster Abbey in April 1603. On top of her coffin is a crowned effigy.

A canopy over the coffin was carried by six knights, and the banners by 'gentlemen pensioners of the court'.

FAMOUS PEOPLE OF TUDOR TIMES

John Cabot, 1450-98, was an Italian sailor who settled in Bristol in 1490. He tried to find a route to China by crossing the Atlantic, and in 1497 reached the coast of North America. Many of his trips were paid for by Henry VII.

William Cecil, 1520-98, was Elizabeth I's chief advisor for many years (see page 18).

William Cecil

Thomas Cranmer, 1489-1556, wrote many of the prayers in the Book of Common Prayer during the reign of Edward VI (see pages 16, 17).

Thomas Cromwell, 1485?-1540, was Lord Chancellor for Henry VIII (see pages 12, 13, 14).

John Dee, 1527-1608, was Elizabeth I's Astronomer Royal (see page 35).

Francis Drake, 1540?-96, was one of the most famous Elizabethan privateers and was the first Briton to sail round the world (see pages 39, 40, 41).

Robert Dudley, 1532?-88, Earl of Leicester, one of Elizabeth I's favourite courtiers (see page 18).

Gerald Fitzgerald, who died in 1583, was the Earl of Desmond. He was constantly feuding with another Irish family. When Elizabeth I tied to stop this, Fitzgerald rebelled against her too.

Martin Frobisher, 1535-94, was a privateer. He also explored various new sea routes (see pages 38, 39).

Humphrey Gilbert, 1539?-83, was a soldier, explorer and navigator. He discovered Newfoundland, and then tried to set up the first English colony in North America, at St. John. The colony failed, and Gilbert's ship sank on the voyage home.

William Gilbert, 1540-1603, was Elizabeth I's doctor and wrote books on science and medicine (see page 35).

Thomas Gresham, 1519?-79, was a merchant who advised the monarchs on finance. He set up Gresham College in London to teach trading skills.

Lady Jane Grey, 1537-54, was made queen when Edward VI died, by Lords who did not want Mary Tudor to become queen. She ruled for just nine days.

Lady Jane Grey

Nicholas Hilliard, 1537-1619, was Elizabeth I's official portrait painter. He also painted Mary, Queen of Scots and Francis Drake.

Nicholas Hilliard

Hans Holbein, 1497-1543, was a German painter who lived in Switzerland and Italy before settling in England (see pages 10, 14).

John Knox, 1505-1573, was a Scottish minister who was a strong believer in reforming the Church. He is also famous for writing pamphlets arguing that women should not have political power. These were aimed at Mary, Queen of Scots.

Thomas More, 1478-1535, was Lord Chancellor of England during Henry VIII's reign (see pages 12, 13).

Hugh O'Neill, 1540?-1616, Earl of Tyrone, was a Roman Catholic who led a rebellion in Ulster against the English Protestants in 1593. He made peace with the English for a while, but rebelled again in James I's time.

Walter Raleigh, 1552?-1618, was an explorer and privateer (see pages 38, 39).

Edward Seymour, 1506?-52, was the Duke of Somerset, and the first of the Protectors who governed for Edward VI (see page 16).

William Shakespeare, 1564-1616, was the most famous English writer of plays ever to have lived (see pages 28, 29).

Edmund Spenser, 1552?-99, was a poet who was very popular with Elizabeth I. One of his most famous poems, The *Faerie Queen*, is about her. Elizabeth gave him jobs and land in Ireland, where he lived for many years.

Thomas Tallis, 1510?-85, was a musician and composer, who, with William Byrd, was given the monopoly for printing music for most of the reign of Elizabeth I.

Thomas Tallis

Francis Walsingham, 1530?-90, set up the first English spy network (see page 20).

Thomas Wolsey, 1475-1530, was Henry VIII's most important advisor until he failed to get Henry the divorce he wanted (see pages 10, 11, 12).

THE ROYAL TUDORS FAMILY TREE

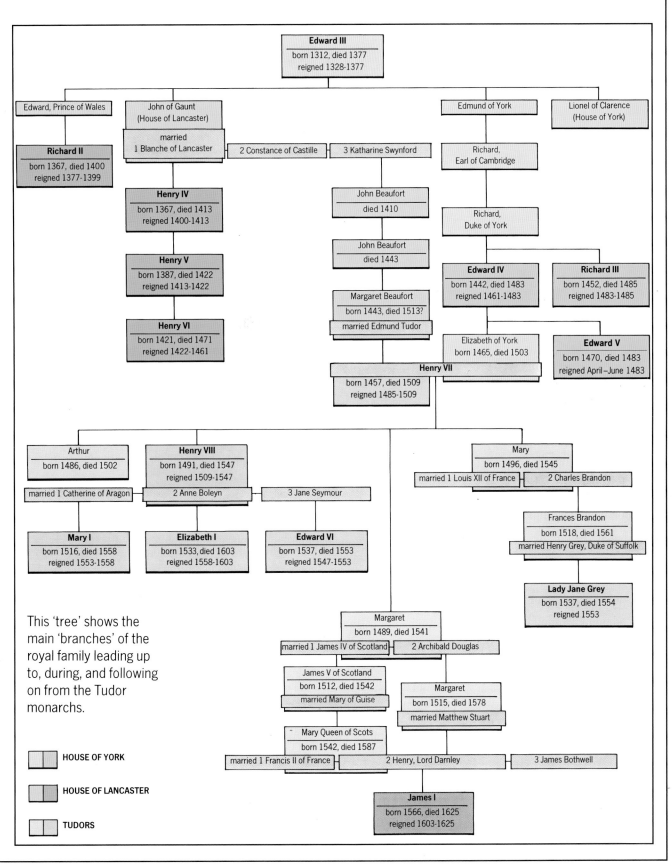

This 'tree' shows the main 'branches' of the royal family leading up to, during, and following on from the Tudor monarchs.

Edward III
born 1312, died 1377
reigned 1328-1377

Edward, Prince of Wales

John of Gaunt (House of Lancaster)
married 1 Blanche of Lancaster — 2 Constance of Castille — 3 Katharine Swynford

Edmund of York

Lionel of Clarence (House of York)

Richard II
born 1367, died 1400
reigned 1377-1399

Henry IV
born 1367, died 1413
reigned 1400-1413

John Beaufort
died 1410

Richard, Earl of Cambridge

Henry V
born 1387, died 1422
reigned 1413-1422

John Beaufort
died 1443

Richard, Duke of York

Edward IV
born 1442, died 1483
reigned 1461-1483

Richard III
born 1452, died 1485
reigned 1483-1485

Henry VI
born 1421, died 1471
reigned 1422-1461

Margaret Beaufort
born 1443, died 1513?
married Edmund Tudor

Elizabeth of York
born 1465, died 1503

Edward V
born 1470, died 1483
reigned April–June 1483

Henry VII
born 1457, died 1509
reigned 1485-1509

Arthur
born 1486, died 1502

Henry VIII
born 1491, died 1547
reigned 1509-1547

Mary
born 1496, died 1545
married 1 Louis XII of France — 2 Charles Brandon

married 1 Catherine of Aragon — 2 Anne Boleyn — 3 Jane Seymour

Frances Brandon
born 1518, died 1561
married Henry Grey, Duke of Suffolk

Mary I
born 1516, died 1558
reigned 1553-1558

Elizabeth I
born 1533, died 1603
reigned 1558-1603

Edward VI
born 1537, died 1553
reigned 1547-1553

Lady Jane Grey
born 1537, died 1554
reigned 1553

Margaret
born 1489, died 1541
married 1 James IV of Scotland — 2 Archibald Douglas

James V of Scotland
born 1512, died 1542
married Mary of Guise

Margaret
born 1515, died 1578
married Matthew Stuart

Mary Queen of Scots
born 1542, died 1587
married 1 Francis II of France — 2 Henry, Lord Darnley — 3 James Bothwell

James I
born 1566, died 1625
reigned 1603-1625

HOUSE OF YORK

HOUSE OF LANCASTER

TUDORS

45

GLOSSARY

alliance an agreement to work or fight together.

banquet a grand meal, with lots of food.

citizens important townsfolk, including merchants and officials who organized the running of the towns.

civil war a war fought between groups of people in the same country.

class the group in society that a person belonged to. In order from highest (richest) to lowest, these were: nobles, gentry, craftsmen, yeomen, peasants, the poor.

constable an unpaid law enforcer, appointed by Justices of the Peace, often old and inefficient.

couriers people who took messages, sometimes goods, from place to place.

courtier someone who was part of the monarch's court and usually lived with the monarch.

craftsmen those who earned their living by a special trade, such as blacksmiths, brewers, bookbinders or bakers.

dissolve to end or break up.

enclosures areas of open field and common land which the landlord fenced in, or 'enclosed', for his own use.

exported sold to another country.

friars religious men who believed in staying poor.

gentry people who owned their own land. Most gentry had their own coat-of-arms, a sign that someone in their family had been knighted.

government the people who ran the country: the monarch, his Privy Council, Parliament and local government officials, such as Justices of the Peace.

heir person who receives someone's possessions when they die, including the right to become the next king or queen.

household people who live with and work for the owner of the house.

Lord Chancellor one of the monarch's most important advisors, responsible for the law courts.

merchants people who made their living by buying and selling things, either in their own country or abroad.

monarch king or queen.

monopoly the right to be the only person to sell or make something.

nobles the rich and important men in the country, who had titles, such as the Duke of Norfolk, and a lot of land. They were closest to the monarch.

Parliament the House of Lords (nobles and important churchmen) and the House of Commons (gentlemen elected by gentlemen) meeting to advise the king. Only the monarch could call Parliament, and no women or people below the class of gentry could vote on who was in the Commons.

peasants people who worked on the land. Some peasants might own a strip of land, but most were just labourers, who worked for the gentry in return for a place to live and some land to farm.

pedlars people who travelled around selling things.

privateer someone who has permission from their monarch to attack the ships of another country and take their cargoes.

rebellion an uprising against the people running the country, to try to replace them.

tournament a contest where knights showed their skill at fighting and riding.

vagrant person with no home and often no job.

watchman someone hired to walk the streets at night, watching for robbers and calling out the time.

yeomen farmers who owned their own land, and who were often rich enough to employ servants.

PLACES TO VISIT

Here are some Tudor sites or museums of Tudor interest to visit. Your local Tourist Office will be able to tell you about other places in your area.

Berwick-on-Tweed Tudor castle and town walls.
Burghley House, Cambridgeshire The Cecil family lived here. Good for buildings, daily life and the Cecils.
Castle Acre Priory, Norfolk Ruins of a dissolved priory.
Elizabethan House, Plymouth Examples of daily life, furniture and homes.
Geoffreye Museum, London Rooms of various times re-created.
Glastonbury Abbey, Somerset Ruins of a dissolved Abbey.
Hampton Court, near London Home of Cardinal Wolsey, then owned by Henry VIII. Has a famous maze.
Hardwick Hall, Derbyshire Good example of grand Elizabethan house style.
Hever Castle, Kent Anne Boleyn lived here. Good for building and for Anne and Henry VIII.
Holyrood Palace, Edinburgh Home of Mary, Queen of Scots for some time.
Jesus College Oxford Set up as an extra college for the University in 1571.
Knole, Kent Good for the study of daily life of important gentry.
Little Moreton Hall, Cheshire Fine example of 'half-timbered' buildings.
Longleat House, near Warminster Good example of Elizabethan building style.
Museum of London, London Wall Models and exhibits, many things from the time.
National Maritime Museum, Greenwich Paintings of ships and also globes and navigational instruments of the period. Also several paintings relating to the Armada.
National Portrait Gallery, London Many paintings from the time, including all the monarchs.
The *Mary Rose*, Portsmouth A ship sunk in the reign of Henry VIII. Examples of everyday things and weapons.
Ormondes Castle, Tipperary, Eire An Elizabethan manor house, thought to be the birthplace of Anne Boleyn.
The Red Lodge, Park Row, Bristol Tudor house, examples of daily life.
Rievaulx Abbey, Yorkshire Ruins of a dissolved abbey.
Stratford-on-Avon Shakespeare's birthplace.
Tintern Abbey, Gwent Ruins of a dissolved abbey.
Tower of London Many people were imprisoned there. Good collection of armour and weapons.
Tudor Merchant's House, Quay Hill, Tenby, Wales An early Tudor town house.
West Stowe Hall, Sussex Good examples of daily life.
Westminster Abbey Crownings and burials of monarchs.
Yarmouth Castle, Isle of Wight Good example of the defenses built by Henry VIII.

INDEX

Abbey
    Glastonbury 14
    Rievaulx 14
    Tintern 14
Act of Uniformity 16
America 22, 32, 38, 39, 40
Aragon, Catherine of 6, 12, 13
Armada, The Spanish 25, 40, 41
army 40
Arthur (son of Henry VII) 6, 45

Battle of
    Bosworth 5, 6
    Flodden 8
Bible 14, 16, 35
Boleyn, Anne 12, 13
Book of Martyrs 17
Burbage, James 28, 29
Burbage, Richard 28
Burghley, Lord 42
Burghley House 30

Cabot, John 39, 44
Cabot, Sebastian 39
Castle Acre Priory 14, 15
Catholic(s), Roman 10, 12, 15, 17, 18, 20, 21, 40
Cecil, William 18, 30, 44
churches and churchmen 6, 14, 15, 26, 34, 36
Church, the 11, 12, 13, 14
    Catholic Church 10, 13, 14, 15
    English Church 5, 10, 12, 14
    Protestant 15, 17
Cleves, Ann of 13
clothes 24, 25
coal, coal mines 22, 23, 35
coins 23, 37
colonies 38, 39
copper 23, 35

country, countryside 23, 26
Court of Star Chamber 7
court(s) 5, 11, 36
courtiers 19, 45
craftsmen 45
Cranmer, Archbishop Thomas 12, 16, 17, 18
Cromwell, Thomas 12, 13, 14, 44

Dee, John 35, 44
Defender of the Faith 10
Devereux, Robert 43
Divinity 34
Drake, Francis 38, 39, 40, 41, 44
drinks 32, 33
Dudley,
    Edmund 7,
    Robert 18, 44
Duke of
    Medina Sidonia 40, 41
    Northumberland 16
    Somerset (the Protector)16

Earl of
    Essex 43
    Warwick 7
Edward (son of Henry VIII and Jane Seymour) 13
Elizabeth,
    daughter of Henry VIII and Anne Boleyn 12
    daughter of Henry VIII and Jane Seymour 13
    of York 6
Empson, Richard 7
enclosures 11, 26, 45
England 5, 6, 7, 11, 13, 16, 17, 18, 20, 22, 23, 35, 36, 38, 39, 40, 43
English 10, 12, 13, 16, 21, 38, 39, 40, 41
English Channel 40, 41
Europe 22, 32, 39, 43
explorers 38

farms, farmers 25, 26, 30, 32
Field of the Cloth of Gold 9
Fitzgerald, Gerald 44
fleet 40, 41
food 32, 33
Fotheringhay Castle 21
Foxe, John 17
France 8, 18, 19, 20, 21, 22, 23, 32, 43
Frobisher, Martin 38, 39, 44
fur 23, 25, 38
furniture 31

gentry 6, 45
Gilbert,
    Humphrey 44
    William 35, 44
glass 30, 35
gold 38, 39, 40
government 45
Great Harry 11
Gresham, Thomas 44
Grey, Lady Jane 44, 45
guns 35, 40, 41

Hampton Court 10
Hathaway, Anne 29
Hawkins, John 38, 39
Hengrave Hall 19
Henry Tudor 5
heretics 17
Hilliard, Nicholas 44
Holbein, Hans 10, 14, 44
House of Lancaster 5, 6, 45
House of York 5, 6, 45
houses, household 30, 33, 45
Howard,
    Catherine 13
    Lord 40, 41
Hudson Bay,
    Hudson Strait 39

Ireland 5, 43
iron 22, 35

jousting 9
Justices of the Peace, JPs 36

King
    Edward III 45
    Edward IV 6, 7, 45
    Edward VI 16, 45
    Francis I of France, 9
    Henry IV 45
    Henry V 45
    Henry VI 45
    Henry VII 5, 6, 18, 45
    Henry VIII 7, 8, 9, 10, 11, 12, 13, 14, 15, 18, 45
    James I 21, 39, 45
    James V of Scotland, 20, 43
    Philip II of Spain 39, 40
    Richard II 45
    Richard III (of York) 5, 6, 45
King's Council 6, 7, 11
Knox, John 44

Latimer, Bishop Hugh 17
Lionel of Clarence (House of York) 45
London 22, 23, 29, 40, 43
Lord
    Bothwell 20
    Burghley (William Cecil) 18, 30
    Darnley (Henry Darnley) 20
    Howard 40, 41
Lord Chancellor 11, 12
Luther, Martin 10

manor house 26
Marlowe, Christopher 28
Marquess of Pembroke 12
Mary (daughter of Henry VIII and Catherine) 8
Mary Rose 33
Mary Stuart, Queen of Scots 20, 21, 43, 45

merchants 5, 23, 25, 34, 37, 45
monasteries 14, 34
monopolies 19, 45
More, Thomas 12, 13, 44

Netherlands 40
Newfoundland 22, 23
night watchman 25, 37
nobles, noblemen 5, 6, 7, 11, 14, 45

O'Neill, Hugh 44

Parliament 5, 6, 13, 14, 16, 18, 20, 42, 45
Parr, Catherine 13
peasants 14, 37, 45
Pilgrimage of Grace 15
Pope, The 6, 10, 11, 12, 13, 15
Portugal and Portuguese 22, 38, 41
Prayer Book, English 16, 18, 35
privateer 39, 45
progresses 19
Protestant 16, 17, 18, 20

Queen
    Elizabeth I 18, 19, 20, 21, 24, 26, 30, 35, 39, 40, 42, 43, 45
    Mary I 16, 17, 18, 37, 45
    see also Mary Stuart, Queen of Scots

Raleigh
    Walter 38, 39
Reformation 5, 15, 18, 34, 43
Ridley, Bishop Nicholas 17
River Thames 10, 11, 27
Russia 23, 39

sailors 38, 40
schools 34, 35
science, scientists 34, 35

Scots, Scotland 5, 8, 20, 23, 41
Seymour,
    Edward 44
    Jane 13
Shakespeare, William 5, 28, 29, 44
ships 38, 39, 40, 41
Simnel, Lambert 7
Simson, Cuthbert 37
slaves, African 38
Spain 6, 17, 18, 19, 21, 23, 32, 39, 40, 41, 42
Spaniards, Spanish 22, 38, 39, 40, 41
Spenser, Edmund 44
spices 32, 33, 38
Stuart(s) 5, 20, 21

Tallis, Thomas 44
taxes 6, 7, 11
theatres 28, 29
torture 37
Tower of London 7, 27, 37
towns, town houses 22, 23, 26, 27, 37, 30
trade, trade routes 22, 23, 38
Tutbury Castle 21

vagrant 36, 45
Vicar General 14

Wales 5, 36
Walsingham, Francis 20, 21, 44
Warbeck, Perkin 7
Wars of the Roses 5
warship 39
Westminster Abbey 16, 43
wine 23, 32, 33
witchcraft 37
Wolsey, Thomas 10, 11, 12, 44
wool, woollen cloth 22, 23, 25

yeomen 5, 45